THE LITTLE GUIDE TO THE
TOUR DE FRANCE

First published in 2025 by OH
An Imprint of HEADLINE PUBLISHING GROUP LIMITED

1

Disclaimer:

Cataloguing in Publication Data is available from the British Library

ISBN 978-1-03542-264-7

Compiled and written by: David Clayton
Editorial: Saneaah Muhammad
Designed and typeset in Queulat by: Tony Seddon
Project manager: Russell Porter
Production: Marion Storz
Printed and bound in Dubai

Headline's policy is to use papers that are natural, renewable and recyclable products and made from wood grown in well-managed forests and other controlled sources. The logging and manufacturing processes are expected to conform to the environmental regulations of the country of origin.

HEADLINE PUBLISHING GROUP LIMITED
An Hachette UK Company
Carmelite House, 50 Victoria Embankment, London EC4Y 0DZ

The authorised representative in the EEA is Hachette Ireland, 8 Castlecourt Centre, Dublin 15, D15 XTP3, Ireland (email: info@hbgi.ie)

www.headline.co.uk   www.hachette.co.uk

THE LITTLE GUIDE TO THE
TOUR DE FRANCE

Independent and Unofficial

GRUELLING QUOTES

FROM THE MOUNTAINS TO THE CHAMPS-ÉLYSÉES

CONTENTS

INTRODUCTION

One of the ultimate tests of endurance, requiring man and bicycle to be in perfect harmony, all played out against spectacular scenery and steeped in dramatic history.

Established in 1903 by Henri Desgrange (1865–1940), a French cyclist and journalist, the race has been run every year except during the World Wars. Desgrange's newspaper, *L'Auto* (now *L'Equipe*), sponsored the Tour to boost circulation. Two events sparked spectator interest in the race: in 1910 the riders were sent, for the first time, over the treacherous "Circle of Death" in mountain passes in the Pyrenees; and 1919 marked the introduction of the yellow jersey – yellow being the colour of paper on which *L'Auto* was printed.

The Tour de France continued to grow in popularity and has been thrilling people and challenging cyclists for well over a century. It is seen by many to be the pinnacle of cycling achievements. From the controversies to the coloured jerseys and the mountain climbs to the sprints, the Tour de France is one of the most iconic sporting events in the world and makes headline news every year.

With fascinating facts and remarkable stories behind this prestigious and gruelling event, dramatic victories and heart-wrenching defeats, this tiny tome dives into the legendary riders, epic battles and memorable moments, along with the passion, perseverance and perspiration, of this thrilling race.

CHAPTER
ONE

The Grand Départ

The drama and anticipation of the Tour de France is tangible at the start line as the 'Grand Départ' gets underway...

66

Let's organize a race that lasts several days longer than anything else. Like the six-day ones on the track, but on the road. Our big towns will welcome the riders.

99

Géorges Lefèvre

66

If I understand you correctly, petit Géo, you're proposing a Tour de France?

99

Henri Desgrange
As a circulation battle began between sports magazines *Le Velo* and *L'Auto*, *L'Auto* editor Desgrange organised a brainstorming session among his trusted staff to reinvigorate the newspaper and give it an edge. Géorges Lefèvre, a writer who was covering cycling and rugby, came prepared (November 2002)

“

The Tour de France is finished, and the second edition will, I fear, also be the last. It has died of its success, of the blind passions that it unleashed, the abuse and the dirty suspicions... We will therefore leave it to others to take the chance of taking on an adventure on the scale of the Tour de France.

”

Henri Desgrange

In 1904, race founder Desgrange threatens the second Tour de France may be the last after the incredible popularity brings with it bureaucratic arguments and disqualifications as the official body, *Union Vélocipédique Française* (UVF), attempted to wrestle control and impose new rules.

The start of the course is known as the Grand Départ. Since the 1950s this has typically taken place in a different town each year, and since the 1970s it has been common to award the Grand Départ to cities outside France in order to increase international viewers, which often top 500 million globally.

"

I know what it's like
coming back from zero,
maybe even below that.
If all goes well, the next
three weeks, I'll be there
on the start line.

"

Fabio Jakobsen

Dutch cyclist Jakobsen on his preparation for the
2021 Tour de France, "The Grand Départ", *Tour de France:
Unchained*, Netflix, 2023

66

You're assassins!
All of you!

99

Octave Lapize
The 1910 Tour de France winner reprimands race officials after a
new mountain stage of 326 km was introduced, sending riders over
the Peyresourde, Aspin, Tourmalet and Aubisque – four summits
which would later become known as the "Circle of Death",
podiumcafe.com, July 2022

"

I'll tell you what's up, you're criminals, you hear? Tell Desgrange that from me. You don't ask a man to make an effort like this, I've had enough.

"

Octave Lapize
Race winner Lapize continues his tirade against officials – and founder Henri Desgrange in particular, cyclist.co.uk, 2021

"

I can see the Tour in their hearts, and in their eyes. For that, I say thank you to everyone in Yorkshire who has made this Grand Départ so very, very special.

"

Christian Prudhomme

Tour de France director Prudhomme praises the people of Yorkshire as an estimated 2.5 million line the roads for the first two stages of the 2014 race, cyclinguphill.com, 2016

"

The 2,500 km that I've just ridden seem a long line, grey and monotonous, where nothing stood out from anything else. But I suffered on the road; I was hungry, I was thirsty, I was sleepy, I suffered, I cried between Lyon and Marseille, I had the pride of winning other stages, and at the controls, I saw the fine figure of my friend Delattre, who had prepared my sustenance, but I repeat, nothing strikes me particularly.

"

Maurice Garin
Taken from the 1903 notes of the first Tour de France winner,
cycling-passion.com, June 2013

The inaugural Tour de France was held in 1903 over a 2,428 km distance, containing just six stages. Maurice Garin, just 22 years old, was the overall winner with his La Française bicycle, making it officially the first bike to win the Tour de France.

66

I must say that one single thing struck me, that a single thing sticks in my memory: I see myself, from the start of the Tour de France, like a bull pierced by banderillas, who pulls the banderillas with him, never able to rid himself of them.

99

Maurice Garin
Taken from the 1903 notes of the first Tour de France winner,
cycling-passion.com, June 2013

❝

I'll win the Tour de France provided I'm not murdered before we get to Paris.

❞

Maurice Garin

The 1903 champion's words as he attempted to defend his title in 1904, but he was attacked by mobs near Saint-Étienne, who wanted local rider Faure to triumph, onlinebicyclemuseum.co.uk

> I still feel that variable gears are only for people over 45. Isn't it better to triumph by the strength of your muscles than by the artifice of a derailer? We are getting soft... As for me, give me a fixed gear!

Henri Desgrange

In 1925, the man credited as the founder of the Tour de France – former racer and journalist Henri Desgrange – was a hard taskmaster and attempted to make life as tough as possible for riders, cyclinguphill.com, 2016

"

I was nervous before the stage, because this is the one where you can lose the Tour de France. Then I had a problem, I really panicked. We talked about what we do if we have a puncture, or have a crash, but I didn't think about what would happen if I dropped my chain.

"

Jonas Vingegaard

Two-time General Classification winner Vingegaard shows even the best have starting line nerves, "The Grand Départ", *Tour de France: Unchained*, Netflix, 2023

" Just ride. Just ride. Just ride. "

Faustino Coppi

Two-time Le Tour champion Coppi responds to the question of how
to become a champion (1952), dahlquistcycleworks.com

> **"**
>
> France is not unaware that, without the war, the crack rider from Anderlecht would be celebrating not his third Tour, but his fifth or sixth.
>
> **"**

Henri Desgrange

Tour de France supremo Desgrange acknowledges the brilliance of Belgian rider Philippe Thys, who won in 1913, 1914 and 1920 – with only the First World War denying him more triumphs, capovelo.com, October 2024

Since the first race in 1903, the Tour de France has only been suspended for World Wars in 1915-18 and 1940-46. During the COVID-19 pandemic the race was allowed to continue within strict guidelines for riders, teams and spectators.

66

The only words of French he could manage were: 'No bananas, lots of coffee, thank you.'

99

Henri Desgranges

Desgranges talks of 1924 winner Ottavio Bottecchia – and the Italian's problems with speaking French! *La Fabuleuse Histoire du Tour de France*, Pierre Chany, 1988

"

Not tired, French and Belgians good friends, cycling good job.

"

Ottavio Bottecchia

Bottecchia, a man of few words, would win in 1924 and 1925 and had learned enough French to express himself after his first win – just about! Transportationhistory.org

> **"**
>
> Marc Madiot is like a protective dad. He's the father of the family, the Groupama-FDJ family. And he defends us like a mother hen defends her chicks. He shields us. He's never let us down.
>
> **"**

Thibaut Pinot
Former Groupama-FDJ rider and French racing idol Pinot reflects on one of the sport's most respected team managers... "The Weight of a Nation", *Tour de France: Unchained*, Netflix, 2023

The first two editions of the Tour de France were mostly raced around a flat circuit. In an attempt to make the race more exciting, in 1905 the Tour's first major climb was introduced – the Ballon d'Alsace. As a result, riders were permitted to change their fixed-gear bikes at the base and again at the summit, so they had appropriate methods of climbing and descending. France's René Pottier reached the top first, making him the first King of the Mountains in Tour history – though this was an unofficial title at that stage.

"

It is a stage set for the sort of riders who are in peak form. The ones who, on the start line, are at 100 per cent condition.

"

Bernard Hinault

Five-time champion Hinault on the Grand Départ from Yorkshire – and what's needed to compete to win the Tour, roadcycling.com, March 2014

66

For a rider to win this Tour, they know they can't just turn up and be at 60-90 per cent level. It will be a very exciting stage, and very challenging.

99

Bernard Hinault

More on the high standards needed to succeed, roadcycling.com, March 2014

"

I no longer recognised him. He had been liberated; Louison the worrier had become a warrior.

"

Jean Bobet

Louison Bobet's brother, Jean, reflects on Louis' 1954 Tour
win – he would become the first man to win three successive Tours,
cyclist.co.uk, September 2020

"

[Eddy] Merckx was
the greatest, but
Bernard [Hinault] was
the most impressive.

"

Lucien Van Impe
on Hinault's legendary status, *The Badger: Bernard Hinault and the
Fall and Rise of French Cycling*, William Fotheringham, 2015

"

Let's finish together... Let me win the stage. Tomorrow you will win the Tour.

"

Gino Bartai

Defending champion Gino Bartai and Italian compatriot
Fausto Copp showed amazing camaraderie in the 1949 Tour, with the
ageing Bartai securing one last triumph before the younger Copp
took his title, bicycling.com, 2019

The rider who finishes
last in the General
Classification – the
name for the category
that decides the overall
winner – is known as
The Lanterne Rouge or
'Red Lantern'. The phrase
draws its inspiration from
the red lantern that hung
on the last carriage of
a train, signalling that
no part of the train was
missing.

The first Grand Départ to take part outside of France was in 1954 in the Netherlands. Starting in Amsterdam, Dutch native Wout Wagtmans won stage one to Brasschaat, delighting home fans and expanding the wider appeal of the Tour. It was also the first Tour with a team time trial.

> **"**
> # The day when I start a race without intending to win it, I won't be able to look at myself in the mirror.
> **"**

Eddy Merckx
Merckx on his winning attitude, *Half Man, Half Bike: The Life of Eddy Merckx, Cycling's Greatest Champion*, William Fotheringham, 2013

CHAPTER
TWO

Blood, Sweat & Gears

Training, racing and finishing – there are few more demanding tests of endurance than the Tour de France...

66

There's honour in suffering, in digging deeper than you thought possible and carrying on against screams of protest from every part of your body. It shows rivals that you can't be broken and team-mates that their work and altruism was not in vain.

99

Jamie Wilkins

Journalist Jamie Wilkins on the mentality needed to win the Tour, "Learning to love pain: life as a Tour de France rider", guardian.co.uk, July 2010

66

It is different to every other race of the year... it's so intense, psychologically, it isn't so much the physical effort. It's the concentration that's required to sustain yourself for four weeks and survive in this environment.

99

Dan Martin
Tour de France stage-winner on what makes the the race
uniquely challenging, esquire.com, July 2019

"

Beyond pain there is a whole universe of more pain.

"

Jens Voigt

Two-time Tour de France winner Voigt touches on the pain
only riders truly know, procyclinguk.com, October 2023

"

When you are in front, when you dominate the others, it's a pleasure.

"

Bernard Hinault
Five-time Tour winner Hinault on his enjoyment of
being in the lead, roleur.cc

The Tour de France takes place over 23 days, with two days' rest included. The longest Tour de France in history was held in 1926, when the racers had to cycle 5,745 km – the equivalent of riding from London to New York!

"They're riding into the abyss of lactic-acid-crippling haze."

Bob Roll

Former-cyclist-turned-commentator Bob Roll
delivers one of his most memorable lines, trailrunnermag.com,
June 2022

"

Make friends with pain, and you'll never be alone.

"

Ken Chlouber

The founder of the iconic Leadville Trail 100 shares his advice for any Tour de France competitor to take on board, trailrunnermag.com, October 2022

"

I lost ten teeth. I had 130 stitches. I lost bone in the upper and lower jaw. I had a lot of cracks in the skull. Maybe I'm forgetting something, but I think that's already enough.

"

Fabio Jakobsen

Dutch rider on his horrific crash towards the end of Stage 1, bicycling.com, 2020

❝

On one hand, this Tour is one of the hardest races that I've never done – actually, the hardest race that I ever did – but on the other hand it was just amazing.

❞

Marcel Kittel

The winner of 14 stages of the Tour de France between 2013 and 2017 looks back on his experiences in the race, road.cc, July 2022

"

Dealing with the pain is one of the biggest talents you need to have as a professional cyclist. Luckily, I like to hurt myself.

"

Wout van Aert
Nine-stage Tour de France winner Belgian racing star van Aert reveals some worrying traits, cyclingweekly.com, June 2023

"

In the moment you're so tired and empty, your legs start to block, your lungs struggle with breathing, you can't hear anything at all.

"

Fabio Jakobsen
A fascinating insight from Dutch rider Jakobsen, "Paris to Paris",
Tour de France: Unchained, Netflix, 2023

"

Three weeks of that kind of intensity — first you have to take into account that they have some kind of genetic predisposition that allows them to be selected for that sport. They have some kind of DNA abnormality or anomaly that kind of self-selects them to the sport. But that said, it is putting yourself through the ringer for three weeks.

"

Dr Stacy Sims
Data analyst and former pro women's cyclist Dr Sims on the uniqueness of a Le Tour rider, sbnation.com, July 2018

" Get me water! "

Tadej Pogačar
The UAE Team Emirates racer's simple request,
cyclingweekly.com, June 2023

In July 1983, German synth band Kraftwerk released the single "Tour de France" due to the quartet's increasing interest in the event and cycling in general. The song captures the joy and speed of the course, as well as the effort and endurance. It peaked at #22 in the UK – but failed to chart in France!

"

There's always moments in a Grand Tour where you think: F***! What am I doing here?! What you do to your body is like some kind of a suicide attempt almost.

"

Jasper Philipsen

Belgian star Philipsen – winner of nine Tour de France stages – succinctly describes the pain and effort that goes into each race, "Plan B", *Tour de France: Unchained*, Netflix, 2023

> **"**
>
> It says a lot about pro cyclists that many retire and then take up triathlons, for fun.
>
> **"**

Jamie Wilkins

Wilkins on the extreme physicality needed, "Learning to love pain: life as a Tour de France rider", guardian.co.uk, July 2010

"

If you don't have the mental strength, you're not made for this job.

"

Marc Madiot

Revered Groupama–FDJ Director of Sport Madiot tells it how it is,
"Plan B", *Tour de France: Unchained*, Netflix, 2023

"

Yes, there are going to be some tough times ahead but if you pull together, work together, our strength is what we have inside of us.

"

Marc Madiot
"Everything for the Podium", *Tour de France: Unchained*, Netflix, 2023

"

Pain is still the friend that always tells me the truth.

"

Chris Froome

British Tour de France champion Froome on listening to your body, velo.outsideonline.com, October 2023

66

I think the crowd was something special. It was not a disappointment – it's just bike racing. I gave everything to be in the break and was grateful I could do my best.

99

Ben Healy
British rider Healy keeps it real after picking up the Combativity Award in the 2024 Tour de France, letour.fr, July 2024

> **"**
>
> An amateur should think long and hard before attempting one of these Tour de France stages. Two would probably necessitate visiting a doctor, and three would require a psychiatrist – any more and you should be checking if that person has written a will!
>
> **"**

Bernard Hinault

Five-time Tour de France winner Hinault warns those physically and mentally not equipped for the race to think twice before entering, velosock.com, August 2021

"

I've always had this idea that if you're going to try something, if you're going to expend that first big block of effort and energy to participate – whether it's riding the Tour de France or applying for a new job or coaching your daughter's soccer team – you might as well go ahead and give whatever else it takes to win. I mean, I'm going to be there no matter what, right? Why not go ahead and get the victory?

"

Johan Bruyneel

Former Belgian rider Bruyneel adopts a simplistic view on giving it your all, *We Might As Well Win*, 2008

"

You have to pick yourself up after the disappointment and just find the motivation again.

"

Jasper Philipsen

Philipsen on finding the motivation to keep going,
cyclingweekly.com, June 2023

66

When you're the oldest rider at the Tour de France, you really feel it.

99

Jens Voigt

German racer Voigt – a two-time stage winner – reflects on one thing nobody can outrun: time, road.cc, June 2013

66

You have to have the pain tolerance of a marathon runner. But then you have to be lucid enough, because this isn't just a sport of pushing yourself, this is a chess game on wheels.

99

Jonathan Vaughters
Manager of UCI WorldTeam 'EF Education' Vaughters
sums up the demands of the Le Tour perfectly, "Attack, Counter
Attack", *Tour de France: Unchained*, Netflix, 2023

"

So I had a little chat with my body. What I don't have is freshness, a sprint, and I don't have a punch anymore. What I do have is a big diesel engine, the desire to go, and the ability and willingness to suffer for a long time.

"

Jens Voigt

German Tour favourite Voigt – never without a smile or a comment, cyclingquotes.com, July 2014

" Shut up, legs! "

Jens Voigt

Voigt explains how he bats off pain and doesn't
listen to his body with one of his most famous quotes,
velo.outsideonline.com, December 2020

" After a really big crash, especially with an injury, some riders get right back on the bike and some need time to prepare themselves mentally for coming back. The healing process is 50 per cent physical and 50 per cent psychological. And some riders, really, they never can get back to the fullest. They just never make it. The fear is just too much. **"**

Helge Riepenhof
Team HTC-Columbia doctor on the often devastating effects
of a crash in Le Tour, nytimes.com, May 2010

66

I can do all the
important things in
life. I can eat sushi.
And I can sign the
credit card bills for
my wife.

99

Jens Voigt

After an horrific crash, Voigt quickly makes light of his
pain, nytimes.com, May 2010

"

Crashing, as we
are all aware of, is
not a very pleasant
experience. Everybody
is scared of it, no
matter who they are.

"

Jens Voigt
On a scary risk in cycling, nytimes.com, May 2010

"

Diagnosis of two small fracture took me by surprise. Shows how powerful the mind is in pushing through. No wonder I couldn't stand up straight!

"

Dan Martin

Irish rider Martin takes a career-best sixth place and later discovers he'd been riding with two broken vertebrae, dailymail.co.uk, July 2017

"

As long as I breathe, I attack.

"

Bernard Hinault
Hinault's tenacity strikes again, bicyclingaustralia.com.au

66

It goes uphill like all the others, doesn't it?

99

Bradley Wiggins

A characteristically nonchalant Wiggins ahead of two
punishing days in the Pyrenees, si.com, July 2017

"

I'm just trying to soak it all in. You never imagine it will happen to you but it's amazing. I still look back and think: 'How did I win the Tour, going day to day under that pressure?'

"

Bradley Wiggins
Wiggins speaking after his 2012 victory, independent.co.uk,
July 2024

CHAPTER
THREE

Myths, Mountains & Magic

The Tour de France has taken on an almost mystical aura that both fascinates and inspires those who compete to unheralded new highs...

"

It's my life. When I
was a kid, I was called
to cycling the way a
priest is called to
the Church.

"

Marc Madiot
Madiot on his higher calling, "The Weight of a Nation",
Tour de France: Unchained, Netflix, 2023

> **"** At altitude, in the mountains, you discover some new kind of feeling. You have to be ready. **"**

Primož Roglič

Slovenia's Roglič – a three-time stage winner - on hitting new heights, cyclingnews.com, May 2023

"

Tomorrow will be a short stage, and I feel comfortable at altitude, so it's not a problem for me. There may be fireworks, but either way it's the legs that will do the talking, there will be no secrets.

"

Remco Evenepoel

Belgian Olympic gold medallist Evenepoel and his talking legs,
letour.fr, July 2024

" This Mountain jersey is prestigious. "

Richard Carapaz
Polka dots never looked so good for the 2024
King of the Mountains winner Carapaz, letour.fr, July 2024

"

On a mountain ascent, pain shows who you are.

"

Marc Madiot
More tough words from Madiot, "Attack, Counter Attack",
Tour de France: Unchained, Netflix, 2023

> **"**
> The peloton is moving, it never stops. If you're in the peloton, you're alive. If you're not in the peloton, you are facing death.
> **"**

Marc Madiot
Madiot explains the power of the peloton, "The Grand Départ",
Tour de France: Unchained, Netflix, 2023

"

There's only one of the kind that can sprint and climb and ride on the cobbles, and that's Wout.

"

Grischa Niermann

Former racer Niermann pays homage to the
man-machine that is Wout van Aert, "Welcome to Hell",
Tour de France: Unchained, Netflix, 2023

"

It was a magnificently imaginative
invention, a form of odyssey in
which the lonely heroism of unpaced
riders was pitted against relentless
competition and elemental nature.
The Tour encompassed the territory
of France, and Desgrange later
claimed that it encouraged a sense
of national identity, establishing La
Patrie in clear geographic terms.

"

Jim McGurn

The Chief Executive of *Cycling Weekly* lovingly describes the
Tour de France and the magic it evokes for riders and spectators,
cyclinguphill.com, May 2016

The mountain passes and hills that form the Tour de France changes each year. The highest peak ever reached is Cime de la Bonette-Restefond, which reaches an astonishing 2,802 m (9,193 ft). It has been used sparingly in Le Tour, in 1962, 1964, 1993 and 2008.

"

I am super happy with my Tour de France: it has been a success. We have grown little by little until finishing the race very well, and that is a great feeling to go home very happy. In Ecuador there are very few top-level athletes, but we have achieved great things. I am very proud to be able to bring this jersey to my country.

"

Richard Carapaz
Ecuadorian rider Carapaz reflects on a superb 2024 Tour
that saw him win three stages, including the Mountains Classification,
letour.fr, 2024

66

Sometimes I feel like I am more popular than I am talented. There are days when I wish I got less love and more wins.

99

Thibaut Pinot

Three-time Tour stage winner Pinot questions his adoring fans and wonders if a trade off between success and popularity would make him happier, "The Weight of a Nation", *Tour de France: Unchained*, Netflix, 2023

"

The French love
Thibaut Pinot because
he's authentic. He's raw,
sometimes too raw for my
taste. He has this ability to
offer something that the
others don't have. Pinot is
a romantic cyclist lost in
the modern world.

"

Marc Madiot

French race boss touches on the enigmatic appeal of one of
his nation's favourite cycling sons , "The Weight of a Nation",
Tour de France: Unchained, Netflix, 2023

"

It's one of the most iconic sporting places on the planet. Even people who don't follow cycling could tell you the Tour de France finishes on the Champs-Élysées.

"

Mark Cavendish
Record Tour stage winner Cavendish shares his love of the Tour de France, "The Weight of a Nation", *Tour de France: Unchained*, Netflix, 2023

"

These guys are really my friends, brothers I would say.

"

Jonas Vingegaard
On fraternity, eurosport.com, July 2022

"

I'm at a loss for words. That was unbelievable. I couldn't believe it when I asked the guys to push hard a little bit, and we were hearing on the radio that the big names were getting dropped. It was textbook from the team, the guys rode such a good race. I'm over the moon to be able to finish it off for them.

"

Chris Froome
The Team Sky rider increases his overall lead with a mountaintop finish in La Pierre-Saint-Martin, cyclingnews.com, July 2015

Spare a thought for Dutch racer Joop Zoetemelk, who holds the record for finishing the Tour de France the most of any rider – 16 all told. Largely because of Bernard Hinault's dominance, he finished second SIX times in the General Classification.

He finally won in 1980 after Hinault picked up a knee injury; without Hinault's domination, Zootemelk could have had the most Tour victories ever.

"

So I flew right over, and next thing
I knew I got to sit in the grandstand,
right in the middle of the big
mishpocha, next to the finish line
near the Place de la Concorde! I felt
ten years old again. To be that close!
Watching all these amazing guys
whoosh by, so fast, in a blur! It was like
waiting outside Yankee Stadium and
suddenly finding Joe DiMaggio!
It gave you a big kick in the heart.

"

Robin Williams

The much-missed comedy actor Robin Williams – a confirmed
Tour de France fanatic – on his VIP experience in Paris,
The New Yorker, August 2000

> 66
>
> To watch a whole stage is a commitment... it's exhausting, but it's also great. It's the only way to really get pulled in.
>
> 99

Ben Stiller

Hollywood star Stiller – a confirmed Tour de France addict, bicycling.com, July 2024

"

In the mountains, you don't grow tired; you grow stronger.

"

Nairo Quintana
Five-time stage winner Quintana takes his inspiration
from altitude, cyclingnews.com, May 2017

> "To finish the circle of my career I had the mountain jersey the first year as a neo-pro, also with a crazy breakaway in the first week, and now in my last Tour I have the mountains jersey again. I like that – it's a good story."

Jens Voigt
Voigt ends his Tour de France career in style as the King of the Mountains, cyclingnews.com, July 2014

"

Now that I am officially the biggest climber in the Tour de France I am waiting for a one million dollar contract next year. Hey, I am the best climber in the Tour – yes, I will sign again!

"

Jens Voigt

After securing the mountain jersey once last time,
Voigt invites offers for one last Tour, cyclingnews.com, July 2014

"

They get that close
you can smell the
beer on their breath
sometimes; it is a
bit daunting.

"

Geraint Thomas
Welsh champion Thomas and the pitfalls of the
in your face nature of some of the Le Tour crowds, "Breakneck
Speeds", *Tour de France: Unchained*, Netflix, 2023

66

My mother was there
on the last kilometre
today. She was with me
during the bad times and
I dedicate this day to her.

99

Marco Pantani
The legendary climber dedicates his final mountain victory to
his mother, telegraph.co.uk, February 2004

"

Time-trials are
a sport within a
sport and a really
important part of
cycling that takes as
much mental skill
as physical.

"

Miguel Induráin
On the skill needed for time trials, cyclist.co.uk, June 2023

CHAPTER
FOUR

Legends

The names that will be
forever associated with the
Tour de France – the men
who went above and beyond
to etch their name in
Tour history...

"

The only part of the race I enjoyed was the last weekend... the time trial at Chartres and then riding into Paris as the winner. The rest of the time, I didn't enjoy it. I was the favourite, so every day felt like I was walking a tightrope, knowing that at any second a little crash or a puncture could ruin everything.

So you end up just ticking off the days. Then you have to deal with the media, the doping questions... that is a strain, and you deal with it every day, but it's in no way enjoyable.

"

Bradley Wiggins

British cycling icon Wiggins after securing the 2012 Tour de France – and dealing with the pressures before, during and after, gq-magazine.co.uk, August 2016

66

For me, winning the Tour feels liberating because I don't have to live with the doubts. I know now that I am good enough, and if I never win it again, in a way it doesn't matter. So I can go into it next year with all the self-belief but none of the pressure.

99

Bradley Wiggins

On the liberation that comes with winning, gq-magazine.co.uk,
August 2016

66

It never gets easier,
you just get faster.

99

Greg LeMond

LeMond's perserverance is clear, englishcyclist.com

"

Pain is temporary. Quitting lasts forever.

"

Lance Armstrong
It's Not About the Bike: My Journey Back to Life,
Lance Armstrong, May 2000

"

You become a leader by hurting others.

"

Marc Madiot

Madiot on the brutal truth about being a Tour champion,
"Welcome to Hell", *Tour de France: Unchained*,
Netflix, 2023

" Jonas doesn't know how good he is. "

Richard Plugge

Cycling entrepreneur and visionary Plugge after Danish star Jonas Vingegaard won his fourth career Tour de France stage on stage 11, outsprinting his main rival Tadej Pogačar, "Attack, Counter Attack", *Tour de France: Unchained*, Netflix, 2023

"

It is my hope that revealing the truth will lead to a bright, dope-free future for the sport I love... I hope that all riders who competed and doped can feel free to come forward and help the tonic of truth heal this great sport.

"

Lance Armstrong
Cancer survivor and seven-time winner of the Tour de France
Armstrong – who would later see his titles taken away after a
doping scandal – still remains in many racing fans' eyes
one of the Tour's greatest athletes, skysports.com, June 2015

"

Sometimes I don't know the reason why I attack – even me, I don't know anymore! I guess I was just enjoying the climb, as it was steep and super nice, and I felt like attacking to test my legs into this third week and see if I could get a gap or something.

"

Tadej Pogačar

Three time-Tour champion Pogačar on his ability to
surprise himself, letour.fr, July 2024

"

Today Tadej and Jonas showed that they are the two best riders here. Tadej is even better, he is on another planet.

"

Remco Evenepoel

Rising Belgian star Evenepoel salutes two modern greats after an epic 2024 Tour in which he secured third spot overall, cyclingnews.com, July 2024

"

Training is like fighting with a gorilla. You don't stop when you're tired. You stop when the gorilla is tired.

"

Greg Henderson
Henderson on the brutality of training, cyclingweekly.com,
February 2019

Four riders have won
five Tours each: Jacques
Anquetil of France (1957
and 1961–64), Eddy Merckx
of Belgium (1969–72 and
1974), Bernard Hinault of
France (1978–79, 1981–82,
and 1985), and Miguel
Induráin of Spain (1991–95).

"

He is the best sprinter in the history of the Tour de France, and he wanted to try to win the 35th stage. He is sad, we are sad, the Tour de France is sad.

"

Christian Prudhomme

The director of the Tour de France laments Mark Cavendish's broken collar bone accident as the British cyclist attempted to win a record 35th stage, bbc.co.uk, July 2023

"

I've got to get used to that
(being a legend in the
spotlight), it's going to take
a while. I'm just trying to
soak it all in. You never
imagine it will happen to
you but it's amazing.

"

Bradley Wiggins
Wiggins adjusting to his new fame, bbc.co.uk,
July 2012

"

I'm still buzzing from the Champs-Élysées; the laps go so quick. We had a mission with Cav and we did it. What a way to finish it off.

"

Bradley Wiggins

Wiggins on cloud nine after achieving a boyhood dream, bbc.co.uk, July 2012

66

I don't know what to say, I've had 24 hours for it to soak in.

99

Bradley Wiggins

It'll take time for Wiggins to adjust to his new reality, bbc.co.uk, July 2012

"

There are no races. Only lotteries.

"

Jacques Anquetil
Between 1957 and 1964, Anquetil secured a record five
Tour de France victories as well as 16 stage wins. He is considered
one of the Tour's all-time greats, bikeraceinfo.com

> " To prepare for a race there is nothing better than a good pheasant, some champagne and a woman. "

Jacques Anquetil
A unique approach to race preparation, cyclist.co.uk,
December 2023

66

You can't ride the Tour de France on mineral water.

99

Jacques Anquetil
More of Anquetil's advice, theguardian.com,
September 2017

"

That final Tour win in 1985 sums Hinault up, really... It was Hinault through and through – courage, talent and stubbornness.

"

Richard Moore

The author of Hinault's biography is full of praise for Hinault's ability, cyclingnews.com, November 2011

"

Ride as much or as little, or as long or as short as you feel. But ride.

"

Eddy Merckx

Between 1969 and 1974, Belgian rider Eddy Merckx dominated the Tour, winning a record-equalling five times as well as holding the stage win record of 34 until Mark Cavendish beat it in 2024, bicycling.com, June 2017

66

Don't buy upgrades, ride up grades.

99

Eddy Merckx
The legend is full of good advice, bikeradar.com,
October 2019

"

There is joy in victory, it is only natural to celebrate.

"

Eddy Merckx
Even the legends need to celebrate, cyclingweekly.com,
June 2010

66

What will stick with me forever is the support and love from the public through thick and thin, all as a result of riding a pushbike for a living.

99

Bradley Wiggins

As he announces his retirement in 2016, Wiggins pays tribute to his fans, espn.co.uk, December 2016

> ❝
> # You will never see me in this circus again.
> ❞

Bernard Hinault

Five-time joint record Tour winner Hinault says to the race organiser he will not return to race the Tour again after failing to complete a hat-trick of wins. He does return and wins it three more times! *The Badger: Bernard Hinault and the Fall and Rise of French Cycling*, William Fotheringham, 2015

66

Induráin is the best rider of his generation, but he has won this Tour quietly, without great opposition. If the opposition continues to let him get away with it, his reign looks like lasting a long time.

99

Bernard Hinault

Hinault shares his opinion regarding the Tour's greatest racers, citing the humble Spaniard Miguel Induráin – himself a five-time champion – as perhaps the GOAT, *Reader's Digest*, 1999

66

What you saw on the outside was pretty much what was on the inside too. I had faith in my training and preparation so once I was in the race I was focussed on the job. I didn't have anything else going on in my head.

99

Miguel Induráin
The Spaniard was considered the calmest, if not the greatest, of all Tour legends, cyclist.co.uk, June 2023

66

I think there are riders who are good enough to do so but it's about much more than that. Winning five Tours is as much about luck – not crashing, not getting sick, not having a bad day. I had a lot of luck in five consecutive Tours.

99

Miguel Induráin
Humble as always, cyclist.co.uk, June 2023

"Pulling for Cav to break the record."

Ben Stiller
Hollywood star Stiller wills on Mark Cavendish
ahead of his attempt at a record 35th stage win,
@BenStiller, x.com, June 2024

66

I kind of enjoyed today. OK,
I couldn't go easy, I knew if I got to
the top of the climb by a certain
point, I'd be all right for the time
limit, so I just could do that, then
I could just really enjoy it. Enjoy
counting down the kilometres,
see the flamme rouge for the last
time, and see my family across the
finish line – it was very, very nice.

99

Mark Cavendish
The record stage winner savours his final Tour,
procyclinguk.com, July 2024

66

The Ventoux holds a very special place in my heart – that's when I knew I was going to take it all the way to Paris.

99

Chris Froome

Four-time champion Froome on taking the Mont Ventoux stage at
the 2013 Tour de France – and how it inspired him to his first General
Classification triumph, cyclinguptodate.com, November 2024

66

I would be really happy with that, but I mean in terms of actual goals, getting back to the Tour de France and fighting for even a stage win would be for me an amazing way to end my career, with at least a few more battles in the mountains.

99

Chris Froome

The British legend on potentially ending his career in a blaze of glory, eurosport.com, April 2024

"

I inherited that calm from
my father, who was a farmer.
You sow, you wait for good
or bad weather, you harvest,
but working is something you
always need to do. Sooner or
later a rider will emerge who will
win more Tours. In every sport
we have seen how the records
eventually get broken, and
cycling is no exception.

"

Miguel Induráin
Induráin channel his roots to find inner calm, imdb.com

"

It's the worst. When they run – when they run alongside, that's the time when I'm like, 'Oh mate, just stop.'

"

Geraint Thomas
Welsh Le Tour winner Thomas on space-invading fans on the hill climbs, bicycling.com, July 2024

Britain's Mark Cavendish secured a record-breaking 35th Tour de France stage victory in Saint Vulbas on stage five of the 2024 Tour, defying his age of 39 years.

'Cav' had been due to retire at the end of 2023, but decided to give it one more go – it was a Herculean effort by the Isle of Man rider, who became the event's greatest sprinter and one of cycling's all-time legends.

"

I'm speechless, thank you so much. I love everyone.

"

Mark Cavendish

After securing stage win No.35, Cavendish is overcome
with emotion, cyclingweekly.com, October 2024

CHAPTER
FIVE

The Yellow Jersey

Is there any piece of sportswear more iconic than the Tour de France yellow jersey?

Known as *maillot jaune* in France, it is the ultimate goal of every competitor to wear this revered shirt as the Tour leader, but it is a feeling only a select few get to experience in their career...

Different stages of the race are won each day, as well as ending with an overall winner.

These victories result in different coloured jerseys for the winners.

Yellow – This is worn by the rider in first place by the end of the day.

Green – This jersey is known as the 'sprinter's jersey'. Racers can collect points during the race by winning mini challenges, which are added up to decide who wears the green jersey.

Polka Dot – This jersey is for the person that conquers the mountains the quickest.

White – The white jersey is for the best rider under 25 years old who is nearest the front of the race every day.

66

This is a beautiful country, with the finest annual sporting event in the world... and this is one yellow jersey that will stand the test of time.

99

Chris Froome

British Tour champion Froome savours the moment as he
wears the yellow jersey for the first time in 2013 – he would
go on to win the Tour four times, dailymail.co.uk,
July 2013

"

We did such an incredible job
to protect this jersey. We gave
everything we had. We have
really the smallest budget of the
World Tour teams, so to have
three incredible victories and the
green jersey, it's just amazing.

"

Biniam Girmay
Eritrean cyclist Girmay – Points Classification winner and
three-time stage winner – salutes the team effort that defied
the odds behind his successes, letour.fr, July 2024

"

Under normal circumstances,
I would be disappointed with
my Tour de France. But, after
everything I've gone through,
I can't be disappointed. I didn't
have a good preparation towards
this race, yet I still managed
to regain a good fitness level.
I would have loved to go a bit
further, but it is what it is. I would
like to come back to the Tour de
France and win it again.

The Tour de France is the race I love the most, the most beautiful one – it just has something special. I believe the yellow jersey is the most beautiful jersey in road cycling.

Jonas Vingegaard
After winning both the 2022 and 2023 Tour de France, he fails to secure a hat-trick of victories in 2024. But he promises to return…
letour.fr, July 2024

> **"**
>
> # Mathieu winning the stage and getting in the yellow jersey at the Tour de France, it was like OK, here we are now.
>
> **"**

Philippe Roodhoft

Team Alpecin-Fenix boss Roodhoft on Mathieu van der Poel's first stage victory and his team's arrival in Le Tour, "Plan B", *Tour de France: Unchained*, Netflix, 2023

> **❝**
> Thank you to all of my team. Thank you to G (Geraint Thomas) for the opportunity, and to all the team for believing in me. I think that today I am the happiest guy in the world. I just won the Tour de France, and I can't believe it.
> **❞**

Egan Bernal
Colombian rider Bernal on his 2019 Tour victory,
bbc.co.uk, July 2024

66

It's slightly mixed emotions, but I can be proud. Two years ago, I was here with my broken collarbone, watching Froome win his fourth, and devastated that I wasn't even able to ride my bike. Two years on, I'm slightly disappointed not to win a second Tour de France, which is crazy. I'm proud of how I managed to get myself in shape.

It hasn't been a smooth run into the Tour. This team is incredible, and it was a pleasure to be a part of. To be part of Egan winning his first of many... and to be on the podium in second is an achievement.

Geraint Thomas

A fine comeback and second spot on the podium at the 2019 Tour for the Welsh cyclist, cyclingweekly.com, July 2019

Midway through the 1919 race, organizers listened to the criticism from the press to somehow make the race leader more visible. They decided on a yellow jersey as the most distinctive colour, and the first jersey went to Eugène Christophe, one of the best competitors of his generation.

> **"**
>
> I'm trying to find other ways to win the tour. Maybe I'll get there, maybe I won't ever get there.
>
> **"**

Marc Madiot
"Road to Paris", *Tour de France: Unchained*, Netflix, 2023

"

To have that
opportunity to go
in and try to win
number five – this
is what dreams are
made of.

"

Chris Froome

Ahead of the 2019 Tour, Froome was keen to draw level with other
legends by winning for the fifth time – sadly a nasty crash saw him
leave the Tour early, bbc.co.uk, May 2019

66

In the Tour de France, every second counts. You must seize every opportunity, take risks, and never settle for second best.

99

Geraint Thomas

Thomas reflects on how cycling isn't just an individual sport after his
2018 Tour victory, velo.outsideonline.com, October 2023

66

It's going to be one of the biggest sporting achievements that an Australian has ever [done]. It's humungous.

99

Matt White
White, Australia's national road cycling co-ordinator, on
Cadel Evan's Tour win in 2011, making Evans the first Australian to
win it, guardian.co.uk, July 2011

> ❝
> We were sort of improvising and enjoying some bike racing. I just sort of managed to find myself in that group and I enjoyed it today. It is really incredible, and I have no words.
> ❞

Jai Hindley
Australian rider Hindley surprises himself and wins Stage 5 of the 2023 Tour de France, bbc.co.uk, July 2023

"

Taking the yellow jersey is, I think, a dream of almost every rider.

"

Mathieu van der Poel
"The Flying Dutchman" realises his dream at the
2021 Tour de France – his only yellow jersey so far, rouleur.cc

"

When you wear it, you're wearing the legend.

"

Advertising campaign by Santini, the brand responsible for making the official Tour de France yellow jersey.

Fabian Cancellara is the racer to win the most yellow jerseys while never winning the general classification. 'Spartacus' won 29 yellow jerseys between 2004 and 2015.

Just **five men** have worn the yellow jersey **50** times or more.

They are:

1. Eddy Merckx (Belgium) **96**
2. Bernard Hinault (France) **75**
3. Miguel Induráin (Spain) **60**
4. Chris Froome (GBR) **59**
5. Jacques Anquetil (France) **50**

As for nations, here are the top 5 yellow jersey-winning countries:

1. France **729**
2. Belgium **439**
3. Italy **212**
4. Spain **135**
5. Great Britain **108**

"

All of a sudden, you're draped in a cloak of gold. Everyone gives you space. You can go where you want in the peloton. Everyone respects the yellow jersey. It's got this aura about it, and it doesn't matter who's in it, you pay your dues. Even if it's briefly, you're put in the pantheon of the greats of cycling.

"

David Millar

Maltese rider Millar delivers a memorable quote on the yellow jersey after his first of four career stage wins, cyclingweekly.com, July 2024

66

I've waited my whole career for that moment.

99

Romain Bardet
French racer Bardet, who had started the day at
100-1 on wearing the yellow jersey, secures his first Tour stage win
in seven years in 2024, cyclingweekly.com, July 2024

CHAPTER
SIX

Sprint Finish

Finish

Thoughts, memories
and aspirations of those who
crossed the line in first...

"

I am super happy. I cannot describe how happy I am after two hard years in the Tour de France, in which we always made some mistakes that cost us the race. This year, everything went to perfection. I'm super happy, it's incredible.

"

Tadej Pogačar
2024 Tour de France winner soaks in the moment
after crossing the line and securing his greatest moment yet,
letour.fr, July 2024

66

I still find it weird now. If I think back to myself aged 12 running home from school, if you'd have told me then that I'd actually win the Tour, I don't know what I'd do. I'd probably laugh actually.

99

Geraint Thomas
The first Welshman to win the Tour, British cycling legend
Thomas absorbs the gravity of his success, "Attack, Counter Attack",
Tour de France: Unchained, Netflix, 2023

"

The Tour has always been important. If you were to ask bike riders why they took up cycling in the first place, I bet that 90 per cent would say that it was because of the Tour de France.

"

Eddy Merckx

Five-time Tour winner Merckx and his reverence for the event, cyclingweekly.com, June 2010

"

A bunch sprint is like being in a traffic jam at 200km an hour.

"

Tom Steels
"Grand Départ", *Tour de France: Unchained*, Netflix, 2023

"

In the moment
you're so tired and
empty, your legs
start to block, your
lungs struggle with
breathing, you can't
hear anything at all.

"

Fabio Jakobsen
Dutch cyclist Jakobsen on his Tour stage win and the
sprint to the line, "Road to Paris", *Tour de France: Unchained*,
Netflix, 2023

"

The Tour de France is bigger than cycling. And we've done it.

"

Mark Cavendish

Officially the Tour's greatest ever sprinter lets the magnitude of his record 35th stage victory sink in, independent.co.uk, July 2024

66

Sprint stages overall aren't
always the most exciting to
watch; sometimes the action
can seem static, the tactics
inscrutable. But there's little
in sports that surpasses the
thrill of those last few frenzied
kilometres: the catch, the
leadouts and the final dash
to the line.

99

Joe Lindsey

Bicycling.com journalist Lindsey captures the manic magic
of the Tour sprint, bicycling.com, July 2017

"

I kept on believing because the feeling was good. I could start my sprint with confidence and I'm happy no one was able to pass. This was my best feeling so far in the Tour de France. We didn't have the best start, also feeling-wise, some bad luck, but I'm happy we could turn it around. Two stage wins is not a bad Tour.

"

Jasper Philipsen
Belgian cyclist Philipsen shows his sprint prowess in the 2024 Tour – taking his tally to nine stage wins overall, france24.com, July 2024

I call it organized chaos theory.

Ted King
Tour veteran King tries to sum up the sprint madness,
bicycling.com, July 2015

“

It's just incredible,
I finally won the
Tour, nothing can go
wrong anymore.

”

Jonas Vingegaard

Vingegaard takes an optimistic view on life after his Tour win,
independent.co.uk, July 2022

66

So we're happy, it's been successful. Obviously, everything on top of the fifth stage would just be a bonus for us so we try, we try and get through, we try a sprint, to hang on in the mountains and try and get to Nice.

99

Marc Cavendish
Cavendish on taking the Tour one stage at a time,
eurosport.com, July 2024

The Tour de France has not been without tragedy over the years, but despite the enormous test of endurance, sometimes in stifling heat and thousands of feet high, only four riders have met their death during the race.

They are:

Adolphe Hélière (1910)

Francisco Cepada (1935)

Tom Simpson (1967)

Fabio Casartelli (1995)

"

I've come to believe
that making the show
is just as important
as winning.

"

Laurent Jalabert

French rider Jalabert on becoming Ling of the Mountains
for the first time in 2001, bicycling.com, July 2019

"

A badger is a beautiful thing. When it's hunted it goes into its sett and waits. When it comes out again, it attacks. That's the reason for my nickname. When I'm annoyed, I go home, you don't see me for a month. When I come out again, I win.

"

Bernard Hinault

Tour legend Hinault explains his nickname "The Badger" in 2003, *The Badger: Bernard Hinault and the Fall and Rise of French Cycling*, William Fotheringham, 2015

"

I did my best,
maximum, like I
always do, and that
was enough.

"

Tadej Pogačar
Slovenian Pogačar on the second of his three Tour triumphs
to date, espn.com, July 2021

66

I cannot describe
how happy I am.
After two hard years
in the Tour de France,
this year everything
went to perfection.

99

Tadej Pogačar
Tadej Pogačar on his way to Tour greatness after securing a third
win in 2024, letour.fr, July 2024

"

It's unbelievable,
I am super happy
for him. It is great he
has the record alone
and is not sharing it
with anyone.

"

Geraint Thomas
Thomas reacts to Mark Cavendish's historic win, bbc.co.uk,
July 2024

66

I said, 'Mate, if you win this stage just drop your bike and walk away' – but he was like, 'If I win the first one, I'll want to win more.' So he's definitely going to hang around, isn't he?

99

Geraint Thomas
More thoughts from Thomas on close friend Cavendish,
bbc.co.uk, July 2024

66

Everyone has a smile today – even Eddy Merckx. Everybody thought it was too late but him. It is a wonderful story. He is the yellow jersey of the sprinters.

99

Christian Prudhomme

Race director Prudhomme salutes Mark Cavendish's record
35th stage win, bbc.co.uk, July 2024

To be able to complete the race, riders need a continued source of energy. On average, riders consume approximately 5,000 calories per day during the flat stages, and in the mountains, it increases to around 7,000 calories – 126,000 per Tour! Hydration is critical and riders consume about 10 litres (2.5 gallons) of water per day.

"

He's a very good climber but completely mad.

"

Jesús Loroño
Lorono on 1954 team-mate Federico Bahamontes, who rode
up the Col de Romeyere in front and then stopped to eat ice cream
while everyone caught up, espn.com, June 2013

" I love cycling. I am going to keep racing as hard as I can until this body doesn't allow me to anymore. "

Chris Froome

Froome on his drive to continue, medium.com, July 2022

"

Racing career – completed it.

"

Mark Cavendish

The greatest sprinter in Tour history announces his retirement on Instagram, having broken the record for the most stage wins in his final Tour in 2024, bbc.co.uk, November 2024

"

The race is won by the rider who can suffer the most.

"

Eddy Merckx
More characteristically tough words from Merckx,
cyclingweekly.com, October 2017

The 2025 Tour de France will be staged exclusively in France for the first time in five years. Featuring 21 stages, the 112th edition of the Grand Tour starts in Lille and ends in Paris. The 2025 race will also see a return of the Champs-Élysées finale, on the 50th anniversary of its first finish there.

> ❝
> We decided to bring
> the Tour home; it was
> high time after all the
> foreign starts. ❞

Christian Prudhomme
Director Prudhomme on the 2025 Tour de France,
bbc.co.uk, October 2024

66

You sprint and go as hard as you can until you get to the finish and maybe your life changes if you cross that line first, maybe it doesn't if you don't. That is the nature of this race and what makes it so beautiful.

99

Mark Cavendish
Cavendish on the uniquely life-changing nature of the Tour, standard.co.uk, July 2024

66

The battle between me
and Jonas for the yellow
jersey has been very
special. I think we have
some very interesting next
two or three years ahead
of us. Jonas has stepped
up his game this year.

99

Tadej Pogačar
Three-time winner Pogačar on his healthy rivalry with
Jonas Vingegaard, espn.com, July 2022

"

To win the Tour de France, you must first finish.

"

Fausto Coppi
Legendary Italian rider Coppi, winner of two Tour de France titles
and a nine-time stage winner, with the simplest advice of all in 1952,
cyclist.co.uk, June 2024